Fairy Tale Garage Sale:

Poems of After Ever After

A 30 Painless Classroom Poems book

written by Laura Purdie Salas

educator activities by Colby Sharp

ISBN: 978-1503115323

First Edition - 2014
Cover based on a design by Elizabeth Ferraz

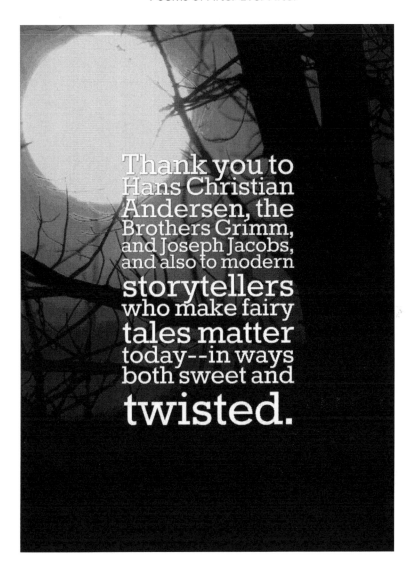

Thank you to Hans Christian Andersen, the Brothers Grimm, and Joseph Jacobs, and also to modern storytellers who make fairy tales matter today--in ways both sweet and twisted.

Table of Contents

INTRODUCTION TO FAIRY TALE GARAGE SALE 9

WHY POETRY MATTERS 18

ABOUT THE SERIES 23

ABOUT THE POET 24

HOW 30 PAINLESS CLASSROOM POEMS STARTED 27

CLASSROOM POETRY TIPS 29

    Sharing Poetry in the Classroom 29

    Sneaking Poems into the Day 35

    Getting Kids Involved 36

    Assessment 36

RECOMMENDED RESOURCES FOR EDUCATORS 38

FAIRY TALE GARAGE SALE: POEMS OF AFTER EVER
AFTER 39

    Huge Fairytale Land Garage Sale – One Day Only! 40

CINDERELLA 42

    Misbehaving Magic Wand 44

    Beautiful Gowns Too Good for You 46

    Out of Time 47

GOLDILOCKS AND THE THREE BEARS 48

    It's Rare! It's Bear! My Price Is Fair! 51

    Up in Flames 52

    Take That, Goldilocks! 53

SNOW WHITE AND THE SEVEN DWARVES 54

    Would It Kill You to Lie a Little? 56

    Touched by Snow White 57

Don't Call It a Coffin! 58

RAPUNZEL 60

No Use for Ribbons 62

This Diamond Sparkles Like Her Shiny, Bald Head 63

Charming Castle – Perfect for One 64

JACK AND THE BEANSTALK 65

Fee-Fie-Foe-Fairian: Surprise! I'm Vegetarian! 68

Solid Gold Sounds 70

The World's Last Magic Bean 72

THE EMPEROR'S NEW CLOTHES 73

Fashion Fit for a King! 75

Seeing Is Overrated 76

Bathrobe, Slightly Tight 78

THUMBELINA 79

Outgrown 81

Daisy Petal Wedding Gown—Unused 82

Fixer-Upper Fly Wings 84

COME AGAIN NEXT YEAR! 85

ABOUT THE EDUCATOR: COLBY SHARP 86

CLASSROOM ACTIVITY GUIDE 88

SCHOOL VISITS 92

THE 30 PAINLESS CLASSROOM POEMS SERIES 93

What's Inside? Poems to Explore the Park 93

Riddle-ku: (Haiku) Poems for Very Close Reading 94

A Need to Feed: Predator and Prey Poems 95

Fairy Tale Garage Sale: Poems of After Ever After 96

Why-ku: Poems of Wonder About the Natural World...........97

Wacky, Wild, and Wonderful: 50 State Poems 98

INVITATION TO SHARE YOUR STORIES 99

CREDITS AND INFO..100

INTRODUCTION TO FAIRY TALE GARAGE SALE

One of the questions kids often ask at school visits is, "How long does it take to write a book?" I feel kind of lame answering with the truth: It just depends. Anywhere from two weeks to several years.

Finding the right audience for a work, and tailoring the writing TO that audience, is a fine art. When I started this project, the poems that came out were angsty and young adult. But there were already books that reimagined fairy tales for teens. I decided I wanted to go younger. Much younger. Preschool age! They love fairy tales. But then I realized my sense of humor and the puns I enjoy using just aren't right for preschoolers. They don't have the facility with language yet to find my humor funny. So then I moved up to 3rd or 4th grade as kind of my ideal audience age. (These poems can still work for younger and older, depending on the reader and the educator that's sharing the poems.)

I also had to think about prior knowledge. At first, I assumed everyone would know these fairy tales. Dumb assumption. Not all kids get exposed to fairy tales. And what about students who come to the United States from other places? They might be unfamiliar with the American version of various tales. So I decided to do a short summary poem to introduce each fairy tale. Good thing, too. As I researched the fairy tales, I discovered many elements that I had never heard or had long since forgotten.

I thought it might be fun to share this project's evolution by scouring my journals to see what I wrote about it. The timeline just shows you the graphic highlights, while the text following it shares actual excerpts from my journals.

Despite the long process and marketing setbacks, I had an absolute blast writing these! I hope you'll have just as much fun reading them.

--Laura Purdie Salas

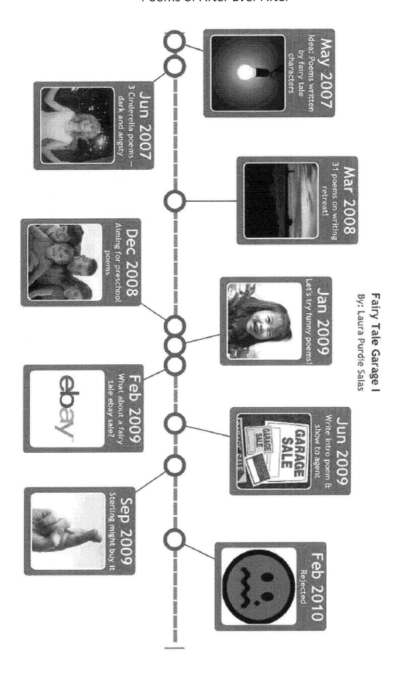

Fairy Tale Garage I
By: Laura Purdie Salas

May 2007
Idea: Poems written by fairy tale characters

Jun 2007
3 Cinderella poems – dark and angsty

Mar 2008
31 poems on writing retreat!

Dec 2008
Aiming for preschool poems.

Jan 2009
Let's try funny poems!

Feb 2009
What about a fairy tale ebay sale?

Jun 2009
Write intro poem & show to agent

Sep 2009
Sterling might buy it

Feb 2010
Rejected

Fairy Tale Garage Sale

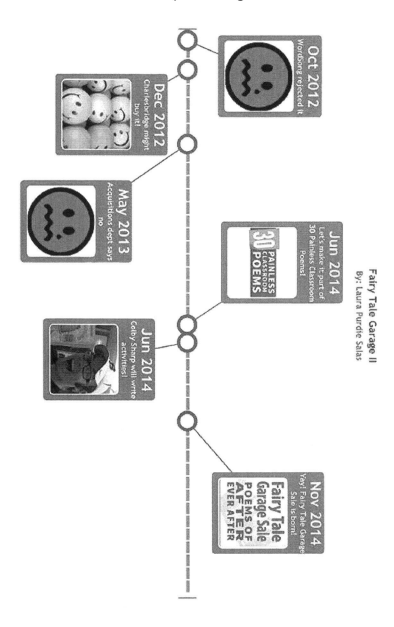

Fairy Tale Garage II
By: Laura Purdie Salas

Oct 2012 — Wordsong rejected it

Dec 2012 — Charlesbridge might buy it!

May 2013 — Acquisitions dept says no

Jun 2014 — Let's make it part of 30 Painless Classroom Poems!

30 PAINLESS CLASSROOM POEMS

Jun 2014 — Colby Sharp will write activities!

Nov 2014 — Yay! Fairy Tale Garage Sale is born!

Fairy Tale Garage Sale POEMS OF AFTER EVER AFTER

EXCERPTS FROM MY JOURNALS

(XXXXXX means it is a project or person I didn't want to name publicly.)

May 31, 2007 - Oh, major idea. Poems that are from fairy tale characters to and from each other. LOVE this idea. This is what I want to work on next. Happily Never After. Oh, I just got excited and itching to write just thinking about that. I'm twitching for a pen. But it will need to percolate in my head for a while. This, though, would be something I could work on in Georgia without lugging reams of research with me! OK, I'm am sparked by this idea. The prince who was a frog before could still have a bad habit of eating flies. Cinderella's prince could complain that she spends all her time shopping for shoes. This could even be aimed at 4th-6th graders. After the Happy Ending kind of thing. Sarcastic or funny poems about the problems these characters face after the story ends. Oh oh oh oh. I can't wait to get started on these. This will be my reward after I turn in XXXXXX to XXXXXX!

June 5, 2007 - So my fractured fairy tale poems. For Cinderella, I have a few ideas, so I'll start with that one this morning.

• One of the stepsisters being more sympathetic character

• Prince Charming complaining about Cinderella's shoe habit

• Cinderella has nightmares about the clock striking twelve

I think it would be cool to do 3-4 poems surrounding each fairy tale. End up with 30-40 poems.

June 7, 2007 - Mary [a critique partner] referred to it as a novel, and in an email afterward, too, but ack—it's not a novel. I want it to be a series of poems, a poem cycle, or whatever name it wants to have, but a series of poems about the same event from several viewpoints. I'm thinking 3 poems for each fairy tale. Will some be light and funny? Or only dark humor? The three Cinderella ones are all pretty dark and depressing, actually. I wonder if an entire book of those would be just too much. Or if not depressing, they're at least kind of sad.

Ooh, in the Cinderella one, I want to use the 12 BONGs of the clock in the poem somehow, increasing the sense of dread with each one, until she wakes up with the final one.

Also, I need to make sure the poems are specific. An event, a single thing. At least for the most part. I don't want it to come across as a summary or an overall, general reaction to the whole events of the fairy tale. General is death to poetry. I have to make sure I focus in on a specific moment. So Prince Charming's poem could start with him discovering Cinderella on the closet floor...Cinderella's could describe ONE typical night where the clock striking twelve instills terror in her, etc.

March 27, 2008 - So many poetry projects I'd like to work on: camp, a Scotland collection, fairy tale garage sale, which I think has enormous potential, teen fairy tale angst poems...

October 24, 2008 – It's been a lovely retreat...I was either writing/working or totally vegging. Nothing much in between. Driving full speed or gassing up. I feel like I did about a month's worth of poetry writing, though! 31 rough drafts for a complete Fairy Tale Garage Sale first draft? WOW! I am SO psyched about that.

December 16, 2008 - One of the things was to look at Fairy Tale Garage Sale. I did, and reread my notes, etc. I feel strongly that I'm going to have to include brief descriptions (very brief) of each Fairy Tale, and then 2-3 short poems (would like to keep them between 2 and 12 lines each) about main characters in each story. I reread everything, and marked a number of very weak entries. There are a few very strong ones, and most are in the middle—decent premise, but needing lots of work to add poetic characteristics and also to make them funny or clever. I think this needs to be funny. I usually go for a mix of moods, but if this is for preschoolers, I think I need to keep it humorous. Even if the poem's narrator is sad or angry or whatever, the poem itself could present that in a funny way. So I'll continue to work on that. I'd love to actually have a version to show XXXXXXX by the end of January.

January 26, 2009 - I've decided I want to make FTGS all funny. No sighing, serious poems. Even if the character itself is angry, like the stepsisters, or sad, like the jilted toad, the poems themselves will be funny because the emotions will be over the top. THAT's the direction I want to take this collection in...I'll save the angst for the teen collection of Not So Happy Endings.

February 9, 2009 - I've been trying to keep this young, but I don't think it's working. The humor is kind of sly, and I think it needs to be more like 3rd-4th grade... It's just not cutting it at the youngest picture book age. But is there a market at the slightly older age? I have no idea. Sigh. But that's the age it's coming out at, so I need to just run with it.

April 27, 2009 - I'm trying to not place high writing expectations on myself, but I also know I have lots of materials to work on this next week: flyers, Rhyme Time course materials, etc. So I'll do what I can. Maybe it will be easier to work on non-creative stuff than to try to work on Fairy Tale Garage Sale. I'm not even going to mess with that while I'm out of town. Just letting it simmer.

June 2, 2009 - I really want to get Fairy Tale Garage Sale off to XXXXXXX for her to decide whether she'd like to submit it around. I think it has such promise, but who knows?

June 11, 2009 - Worked on an intro poem to Fairy Tale collection, so that was good.

September 24, 2009 - And it would be lovely if Sterling would make an offer on FAIRY TALE GARAGE SALE.

February 25, 2010 - Sterling turned down Fairy Tale Garage Sale. I really had my fingers crossed for that. Not only that, but she really liked the ms! Turned it down pretty much solely because of poor poetry picture book sales. So discouraging.

Status Sheet – October 2012 – Pieces abandoned for the foreseeable future - Fairy Tale Poems

October 11, 2012 - Jenn sent me a copy of a really nice rejection from Wordsong (for Fairy Tale Garage Sale) yesterday. Oi. XXXXXXX liked it a lot, but they have something on the same topic coming out.

December 5, 2012 - Found out Charlesbridge might be interested in FAIRY TALE.

June 20, 2013 – Highlight of the conference: XXXXXXX from Charlesbridge telling me how much she loved Fairy Tale Garage Sale. Was sad that she wasn't able to acquire it. Me, too.

WHY POETRY MATTERS

Literature. Grammar. Writing. Science. Math. Social studies. Community. Security. Physical activity. Social skills. Assessment. Test prep. Report cards. Anti-bullying programs. Nutrition. On. And on. And on.

The list of things you are asked to teach or provide to your students keeps growing. How does poetry fit in? And why is it important enough to add into your already bursting days?

POETRY IS ART. Kids deserve exposure to music, paintings, and poetry. It expands their world. And for many students, school might be their only opportunity to explore art.

The job of art is to *EVOKE EMOTION.* It's mysterious and magical--a quick escape from lunchroom drama, math tests, and angry parents. It balances the demands school places on kids and helps kids funnel their own emotions into a size that feels manageable. If a student cries over a poem about a lost kitten, she might be dealing with her fear for her uncle who's serving overseas. And that is a good thing. Giving form and words to kids' fears, joys, and wonders is one of the things poetry does so well.

Poetry is *INCLUSIVE.* As with looking at art or listening to music, every student benefits from hearing poetry. Even poems not in the student's language are meaningful, since poetry is verbal music, full of rhythm and sound. Because poetry is often open to interpretation, kids of all reading levels can enjoy it and make connections with it.

Poetry is *INTIMATE.* It invites readers into someone else's world. When students read poems that touch them, they know there are other people who think like they do. That lets students know they are not alone. Of course, different poems touch and reassure different students, so sharing a variety of poems is crucial.

One of the best things about poetry is that it helps you *SEE THINGS IN NEW WAYS.* It can make you look at a lake, a pencil, or another person--or yourself--in an entirely new way. It lets you imagine a world and life that is different and bigger than the one you've been living in.

Poetry allows you to experience someone else's point of view. Poetry can be a powerful tool in teaching *EMPATHY, DIVERSITY, and TOLERANCE.*

So, poetry is art that is valuable for its own sake, for all the wonderful ways art helps us grow as human beings. But poetry is also practical. It can be a real workhorse in your classroom.

Poetry is awesome for *COMMUNAL READING.* Because of its musical and oral quality, it's perfect for reading aloud and acting out in groups or pairs. It easily accommodates readers of varying reading levels. In an article in *Reading Today* (July/August 2014), fluency expert Timothy Rasinski says that a great way to nurture a sense that a classroom is a team is "through choral reading of poetry, songs, and even cheers."

Sharing poems as an entire class will enrich the body of *SHARED LITERARY TOUCHSTONES* for your students. When students want to travel to the African watering hole from *Dear Wandering Wildebeest* or act out a *Dark Emperor* owl's hunt on the playground, or when they say you remind them of the teacher in *Words With Wings*, you'll know you have created a literary world that connects your students to each other and their world.

Poetry is short, with plenty of white space on the page. It's a song. It's a party. And kids love it. Poetry can be *ESPECIALLY APPEALING TO RELUCTANT READERS,* who find its brevity a welcome contrast to a novel.

Reading poetry helps students *LEARN TO READ.* It enriches their vocabulary. Rhyming poetry helps with their prediction skills. Reading poetry aloud helps improve fluency. And since poetry is short, students can be exposed to all sorts of moods, voices, structures, and forms for a relatively small time investment.

Poetry *INSPIRES KIDS TO WRITE.* The lack of right and wrong, the infinite choices, and the opportunity for self-expression empower kids of all reading and writing levels to write. A kid doesn't have to be the best speller or the best reader in the class to create fabulous poems. In fact, reluctant readers and writers often dive into poetry with enthusiasm once introduced to it.

"I have found that kids who read and talk about great poems every day develop critical eyes and ears. Their literary criteria develop and become stronger. Their vocabularies for talking about the features of effective writing become stronger. And their writing becomes stronger as they borrow from the poetry they've been reading and loving."

– Nancie Atwell

Poetry supports *CONTENT AREAS.* It can reinforce learning, reframe a nonfiction topic, and provide a break from nonstop prose reading. There are nature poems—great for instilling stewardship of the earth. There are history poems—terrific for revealing the human stories behind textbook events. There are even math poems—awesome for making kids see numbers and processes in a new light! Poetry related to content areas adds depth and meaning to these topics.

Poems can help *MEET MANY ELA STANDARDS.* If you're studying point of view, 3 different poems can quickly showcase 3 different points of view. Poetry as a short text provides examples of everything from voice to commas in a series to descriptive structure.

These are some of the reasons, both artistic and practical, to make poetry a staple in your classrooms. As you dive into poetry, you're sure to discover more!

ABOUT THE SERIES

30 Painless Classroom Poems is a poetry series from award-winning children's poet and author Laura Purdie Salas. Each collection contains 30 short poems organized around a specific topic or form. A Note from the Poet—a sentence or two from Laura sharing a bit of insight into the topic or her writing process—accompanies each poem. Every title includes information about why poetry is important in the classroom, along with simple, practical, do-it-now tips for using poetry in your elementary school setting. Each collection wraps up with a set of creative classroom activities connected to those 30 poems, written by an experienced educator. The activities range from on-the-spot and no-prep required to more in-depth projects, and they include both ELA extension ideas as well as connections to various content areas. The **30 Painless Classroom Poems** series is ideal for the teacher, librarian, or reading specialist who is intimidated by poetry or just doesn't know where to start. Each book is perfect for using in National Poetry Month (April), during a poetry unit, or (best of all) all year long!

ABOUT THE POET

Photo: Katherine Warde

As a kid, Laura Purdie Salas devoured books. Her big sisters, Gail, Patty, and Janet, taught her to read when she was 4, and she read for hours every day, despite constant orders from her parents to "Go outside and get some fresh air!" Since she grew up in Florida, she heard these dreaded words all year long. If she was forced outside, she climbed up to her treehouse or lay on the trampoline, reading. Books were magic, conjured up to entertain her, keep her company, and show her the whole world before disappearing into the library return drop. It never occurred to her that real people actually wrote those books.

College was the first time she considered a writing career. After graduating, she worked as a magazine editor and then an English teacher (and rediscovered her love for kidlit). After moving to Minnesota and having kids, she began to focus on children's writing.

Since then, Laura has written more than 120 books for kids and teens, including *Water Can Be...*, (Millbrook, 2014), *A Leaf Can Be...* (Millbrook, 2012: Bank Street Best Books, IRA Teachers' Choice, Minnesota Book Award Finalist, Riverby Award for Nature Books for Young Readers, and more), and *BookSpeak! Poems About Books* (Clarion/HMH, 2011: Minnesota Book Award, NCTE Notable, Bank Street Best Books, Eureka! Gold Medal, and more). She loves to visit with students and teachers to share her joy in poetry, books, and language. She is also the author of several how-to poetry books for kids, including *Picture Yourself Writing Poetry* (Capstone, 2011) and *Write Your Own Poetry* (Compass Point, 2008).

Laura and her family live in Minneapolis, Minnesota, where it's just a touch cooler than Florida! Connect with Laura--she'd love to hear from you!

Site:
laurasalas.com

Email:
laura@laurasalas.com

Blog:
laurasalas.com/blog

Facebook:
facebook.com/LauraPSalas

Twitter:
@LauraPSalas

Pinterest:
pinterest.com/salaslp/

YouTube:
youtube.com/salaslp

E-letter for educators:
tinyurl.com/pztefbq

HOW 30 PAINLESS CLASSROOM POEMS STARTED

As a children's poet, I visit elementary schools to get students excited about reading and writing poetry. I also talk with lots of teachers and librarians. I've spoken at ALA, NCTE, and IRA conferences, along with many others, where I've given presentations for teacher educators, classroom teachers, and pre-service teachers. At national conferences, we poets end up preaching to the choir. The people who attend our sessions already love and use poetry—which is fabulous! But...we aren't making any poetry converts that way.

At first, I didn't even know we NEEDED poetry converts! But as I spoke at smaller conferences or individual schools, where teachers were required to attend, I discovered that poetry was not universally loved. (Yes, this did shock me.) Talking to teachers who hated, resented, or were intimidated by poetry was really disheartening.

But after every session, teachers came up to say some variation of, "I've always been terrified of poetry, but now I can't wait to use it in my room!" Poetry—reading it, writing it, sharing it with kids—is one of my greatest joys, and I want to spread the poetry love.

I've always tried to do that. I have created (on my own or with assistance) many materials—teaching guides, activity sheets, videos, etc.—to help teachers use my poetry and rhyming nonfiction books (including *BookSpeak! Poems About Books, A Leaf Can Be...,* and *Water Can Be...*). But most teachers, even ones who love my books, never realize those materials exist, because they are not distributed directly with the books.

So I started thinking about creating books *specifically* for teachers: books that would include auxiliary materials right there alongside the poem. Books that would make it super-easy for teachers to incorporate poetry into their rooms. Books that would turn poetry-haters into poetry-lovers. And the idea for **30 PAINLESS CLASSROOM POEMS** was born.

I scoured my own unpublished poetry collections. I wrote new poems. I added Notes from the Poet. I talked to educators with a wide spectrum of opinions about poetry. I considered which tips and information teachers might benefit from. I recruited amazing, creative teachers to write activity guides to go with the poems. And I created these books. I hope you like them. If you're a poetry-lover (long-time or recent convert), I hope you'll share these with your colleagues. If you're a poetry-hater, I hope I can change your mind!

--Laura Purdie Salas

CLASSROOM POETRY TIPS

Sharing Poetry in the Classroom

If you're uncomfortable with poetry, you're probably avoiding using it in the classroom. One of the best things about poetry is also one of the scariest: there's no right answer. That can be so intimidating for teachers who are used to being able to give concrete, definite information to students. But it's OK not to have the "right" answer! In fact, that's part of what makes poetry so much fun! So follow prolific poet and anthologist Lee Bennett Hopkins' advice and forget the DAM method (Dissect, Analyze, Memorize). Instead, embrace poetry and all of its uncertainty. It takes just four simple steps.

Present: Read a poem out loud. Slowly. Repeat.

Ask: Ask students what they thought of the poem.

Listen: Really listen to what the students have to say.

Share: Share your own response to the poem.

Let's look at each step in more detail.

PRESENT

Each day in your classroom, read a poem. Or have someone else read a poem. Maybe you can only squeeze in one poem a week (which is still better than nothing), or maybe you can read a poem several times a day (fabulous!).

1. Choosing a Poem

What poem should you read? The key is variety. If you read the same kinds of poems all the time (sweet, rhyming poems, for instance), then kids who don't like that type of poem will just tune you—and all poetry—out. But mix in some free verse, rhyming, humorous, serious, sad, scary, and silly poems, and you'll keep students on their toes. They won't like every poem, but if you share an interesting mix, kids will pay attention to see what you'll do next. Here are few ways to choose poems.

Connect to the season. Read poems that tie into the current season and weather. Check out *Swing Around the Sun*, by Barbara Juster Esbensen, and *Sharing the Seasons*, compiled by Lee Bennett Hopkins, for two wonderful examples of seasonal poetry.

Pick a poem for a specific kid. Got a student obsessed with bugs? Share a poem from *Face Bug*, by J. Patrick Lewis. Say, "I thought Alex might like this poem." Or maybe you have a student who likes to make up nonsense sayings. Try a Calef Brown poem. This method helps kids see that poems are available for everybody (while understanding that not every poem will appeal to every kid).

Tie in with a content area. When you're studying life cycles, read *Toad by the Road*, by Joanne Ryder, and follow (in poems) a year in the life of a toad. Making connections between different disciplines helps show that poetry is simply a way to see and respond to the world—that it can be connected to anything!

2. Reading a Poem

If you're a ham, great! But if you're not, these simple tips will help you hone your poetry skills.

Practice. Read the poem out loud in private a couple of times before you present it to the classroom. This will help you pick up the rhythm of the poem and allow you to present it more smoothly.

Read slowly. The rich language of poetry can be a lot to absorb, so read more slowly than you would read a story or article.

Repeat. Because poetry is not always literal, it can take several exposures before kids totally absorb it. Read a poem twice. And don't be shy about repeating poems from day to day. Sometimes you might have a poem of the week and read the poem every day all week long.

Juice it up. You might not be super dramatic, but small changes can make a poem more effective. Note which words you want to read more loudly or, perhaps, whisper. Can you show the emotion of the poem? This will get easier as you become more comfortable with poetry. If a straight read is all you can manage right now, that's completely fine!

ASK

After you read the poem, ask students what they think about it.

Do you like this poem? Why?

Have you ever felt this way?

Is there a word you particularly like in here?

Who doesn't like this poem? Why?

Does this poem remind you of anything from your own life?

Does it remind you of anything else you've read?

Is there a word here you don't understand?

How does this poem make you feel?

What do you notice about this poem?

You might choose one or two questions, or you might have time for an in-depth discussion. Either way, these open-ended questions will bring forward interesting insights from your students. And if someone doesn't like a poem, no problem! You won't like every single poem, either. Nobody should feel guilty for not liking a particular poem. The point is to start talking about poetry and to encourage kids to have opinions about it. Your classroom will fill up with lively discussions among kids who have lots to say about poems.

LISTEN

Really listen. Don't jump in with your own opinion just yet. Let your students express themselves, and then acknowledge their points with a nod, a smile, a murmur of understanding, or a request for more information.

If a kid says he hates a poem, ask what he hates about it. Don't correct him and say that he doesn't really hate it or shouldn't hate it. Instead, acknowledge his gut reaction, but try to probe just a bit deeper to see if he can put a finger on one aspect of it he really doesn't like.

Helping kids discover what they do and don't appreciate in poems will help them learn to find more poems they love.

As students realize that you consider their opinions valid, they'll get more vocal. They will also quit trying to bait you into defending a poem they don't like.

Of course, you'll want to maintain an atmosphere of polite discussion, where students can disagree with each other and still each feel heard and validated.

SHARE

Your role as a teacher is not to have the right answer about a poem. Your role is to help kids discover and respond to poems! The best way to do that is to model great poetry response yourself. So sharing how you feel or think about a poem is an important part of your poetry time. Consider making this your last step, though, because if you share your response first, your people-pleaser students will simply echo your thoughts. And the students who disagree with your opinion might stay silent, feeling like they were wrong in their response to the poem.

It doesn't do any good to pretend to like every single poem you read in your classroom. If you praise everything, the praise becomes meaningless. But that doesn't mean you should trash any poem. If you do, you'll make the kids who enjoy the poem feel stupid.

Here are just a few sentence starters you can use as you respond to poetry.

This poem reminds me of the time that...

I'm not a huge fan of this poem, but I do really like this phrase from it: _____

This poem makes me feel...

I wish the poet had included _____ in this poem.

I'm a little confused because I don't understand exactly what the poet meant by _____.

Basically, any question you asked your students is a good one for you to answer as well.

Your sharing might lead to more discussion as you and your students search for common ground or try to hash out meaning. The more time you're able to spend on poetry response, both yours and your students', the more insightful, specific, and outspoken your students will become. It just takes some practice for all of you.

Sneaking Poems into the Day

Even in a busy school day, there are plenty of moments when you could pull out a poem to share with your students. Sometimes there will be enough time for a little feedback from students; other times you might just read the poem (twice) and move on to the next activity. You might find it helpful to have a signal that it's time for poetry: a flickering of the lights, a hand clap, or some kind of secret hand signal you and the students agree on.

Here are four possibilities for poeming throughout the day. These are just suggestions. You'll probably find many more opportunities based on your own schedule.

Right after morning announcements: The start of the day can be a great time for a seasonal or weather-based poem.

During content areas: Starting science block with a poem related to your current topic is a no-brainer!

When kids line up to leave for lunch: This time of day lends itself to funny/silly poems, as well as any food-related poems.

After kids gather up their supplies at the end of the day: At the end of the day, the kids are eager to leave. But if you time it right, you can create a peaceful few minutes for poetry. Just don't cut it TOO close to release time, or kids will be watching the clock instead of absorbing the words.

Getting Kids Involved

Want your students to do more than just listen? Excellent! That's the whole idea. After a month or two of sharing poetry with your students on a regular basis, they should be feeling pretty comfortable with it. And then it's time to let them get more involved.

Let kids pair up and find poems to present (or to have you present) to the class.

Post a poem on a bulletin board and have students draw pictures to illustrate the poem. Post their illustrations all around the poem.

Read echo poems. You read a line, and then your students repeat it back to you. Then you move on to the next line. This helps students practice reading fluency, and it works best with rhyming, rhythmic poems.

Get active. Try some of the activities that are shared at the back of this book. They were written by an educator who's busy, like you!

Assessment

In order to devote regular classroom time to poetry, you have to come up with a way to assess students' progress in that area. But how do you assess the students' reading of and comprehension of poetry? The key is to reward students' efforts. Give credit for participation in discussions. Give assignments kids can't do wrong, like choosing a poem to read out loud to the class.

To really instill a love of poetry in kids, they can't fear it. And if they're afraid of doing it wrong, they will fear it. So in the elementary grades, keep poetry assessment very basic. Here are some possibilities.

Ask for volunteers to read poems out loud. This might work best, at first, if kids volunteer to read poems you've already read aloud to them.

Have the students group read poems out loud. Many poems can be read with alternating lines or as a chorus, and it's a great way to get kids up in front of the room in a not-too-scary way.

Give participation points for kids when they answer the questions you ask about poems. Points aren't dependent upon being right or wrong--There are no wrong answers!

The good news is that students who like poetry and have had exposure to a wide range of poems and rich discussions about those poems will be better prepared to not only become lifelong readers of poetry but to perform well on poetry comprehension items on standardized tests.

RECOMMENDED POETRY RESOURCES FOR EDUCATORS

Here are just three resources I recommend. For a more complete listing of resources, please visit my online listing by clicking on the link at 30PainlessClassroomPoems.com:

http://tinyurl.com/nsawdlr

Poetry Friday Anthologies: These anthologies, edited and compiled by teacher educator Sylvia Vardell and poet Janet S. Wong, offer lots of poems, diverse voices, and simple teacher tips for you. I'm proud to have my work included in them and recommend them highly!

http://tinyurl.com/lxh3mo3

Poetry Lessons to Meet the Common Core State Standards: Another wonderful professional book from Georgia Heard, this one is for you if you want specific lesson plans and techniques for meeting CCSS through poetry.

http://www.laurasalas.com/poetry/poetic%20pursuits/poetpurs.html

Poetic Pursuits: These are articles I wrote explaining many common poetic forms. As your comfort level with poetry grows, you'll likely want to know more about it! These articles are mostly about the writing process, though you will also find them handy for increasing your own understanding of different poetic elements, which will be terrific for your classroom discussions.

FAIRY TALE GARAGE SALE:
POEMS OF AFTER EVER AFTER

Huge Fairytale Land Garage Sale – One Day Only!

Come on in! Prepare to buy
from Kings, from ogres in the sky,
from thieves, from queens, from girls gone bald—
prepare to be enthralled...appalled!

Will you buy from Bear or blonde?
Wave a misbehaving wand?
March right through the village square,
In some see-through underwear?

Read the tags—they tell the tale
of why this nifty stuff's for sale.
Choose your treasures. Eat a snack—
but give the poison apple back!

Carry home the things you'll use.
They're priced so cheap, you can't refuse!

Heroes, villains all display
their cast-off goods—but just today!

A Note from the Poet:

I wrote this poem last, even though it's the first to appear. I had my set of poems, but then I thought I needed something to set the scene and explain what was going on. I thought of the big signs I sometimes drive by that are advertising huge neighborhood garage sales and saying what's being sold, and I tried to do something similar here.

CINDERELLA (You Know This Story!)

Life is tragic. Mother's died.

Father weds a wicked bride
whose daughters screech and scheme and scream.
A royal husband is their dream.

Cinderella must stay home
to sweep the hearth and scrub the stone.

But magic, clocks, and one lost shoe
all find their way to "I love you!"

...for guess who!

A Note from the Poet:

Not every kid has heard every single fairy tale. So, at the start of each set of poems, I wrote one poem to summarize the important points of the tale. For Cinderella, those key points seemed to be: wicked stepmother and sisters who dream of a royal marriage, Cinderella having to stay home and clean, and that shoe that leads to Cinderella marrying the Prince. As a writer, always think about what your reader might already know and might NOT already know.

Misbehaving Magic Wand
Item for sale: Magic wand
For sale by: The Fairy Godmother

Wands are for wishing, tapping, waving,

But mine was always misbehaving.

The sky clouded over; I wished, "Umbrella!"

Instead I appeared to—

Cinderella!?

She yearned for a ball at the castle—quite fancy.

I wanted to go, though I knew it was chancy.

A woman my age should not chase Prince Charming.

Believe me, I tried! The results were alarming.

The pale silk gown, blue as May skies,

And crystalline heels appeared in HER size.

Mice became horses, pumpkin turned carriage.

Next thing I knew there was talk about marriage!

I bought a cheap wand at an end-of-year sale,

So my plan for romance was destined to fail.

In my lovely glass slippers, my ball gown divine,

She married the guy who should have been mine!

A Note from the Poet:

In this poem, a lot of the couplets (sets of two rhyming lines) were built around a word I needed to rhyme. I knew Prince Charming needed to be in the poem—of course! So I looked for rhyming words. One option was "alarming." So I thought about what could happen that could be alarming (startling and a bit scary). That led to my thinking about how everything could go wrong for the poor Fairy Godmother.

Beautiful Gowns Too Good for You
Item for sale: Ballgowns
For sale by: The stepsisters

Buy our gowns, our shoes, our jewels.

Buy them all, you stupid fools.

We tried them all—they didn't work!

The Prince chose her. He's such a jerk.

A Note from the Poet:

I love writing poems from someone else's point of view. It can be especially fun to write a poem, a letter, a story, or even a nonfiction piece from the eyes of someone who is totally NOT like me. Here I wanted to capture the mean, spoiled, pouty voices of Cinderella's stepsisters.

Out of Time

Items for sale: Grandfather clock, pocketwatch
For sale by: Cinderella

Chimes and gongs, with their

Loud, rude songs! I want them

Out of the

Castle. I'll

Know the time by the

Sun's steady climb. Forget that midnight hassle!

A Note from the Poet:

I love acrostics. They're one of my favorite poetic forms. Usually, acrostic poems don't rhyme, but I have fun playing with meter and rhyme in them. I especially had fun with castle/hassle!

GOLDILOCKS AND THE THREE BEARS

A brat, a girl, quite impolite
Went stealing in; she had no right!

Two chairs too short or tall in height
But Baby's chair was...just right

Two meals too hot or cold to bite
But Baby's mush was...just right

Two beds, too hard or soft for night
But Baby's bed was...just right

When Bears got home
They had a fright:
A guest that they did NOT invite

Goldilocks slipped out of sight

(and *acted* like she was contrite!)

A Note from the Poet:

One thing that's cool to do in poetry is use repetition. It makes it more fun to read aloud or to even perform in a dramatic way. Since fairy tales already use repetition a lot (often things happen in sets of three), it was a natural fit to repeat "But Baby's…" three times.

It's Rare! It's Bear! My Price Is Fair!
Item for sale: Pottery bowl
For sale by: Goldilocks (Can you believe Mother canceled my allowance?)

Mother keeps saying I should have known better.

But I like adventure! I'm a go-getter!

This rare bear pottery's crusty with porridge.

Just give it a scrub – it's perfect for storage!

I risked my life at a secret location

To bring you this proof of bear civilization.

A Note from the Poet:

For this poem, I thought about what Goldilocks would do after her adventures at the Bears' cottage. And I decided she was kind of a selfish schemer. I can picture her selling things on e-Bay! So she's trying to raise money here by selling a dirty porridge bowl—I love the sharp, harsh sounds of the line: "This rare bear pottery's crusty with porridge."

Up in Flames
Item for sale: Firewood
For sale by: Mama and Papa Bear

We're fuming, livid, cross, annoyed

Our baby's things have been destroyed!

His bed was broken, highchair smashed

All his belongings thoroughly trashed

Take this lumber to build your fire

Ignore that little blonde-haired liar

Girls are gentle? Don't believe

that fib, cause looks can sure deceive!

Note from the Poet:

In the first line of this poem, I played around with synonyms. I always dig around in my own head first, but once I list a few words, I dig out the handy-dandy thesaurus (either in print or online) to find other words that mean about the same thing and get across the mood of the poem.

Take That, Goldilocks!
Item for sale: Blonde curl
For sale by: Baby Bear

One blonde curl

    snatched from thieving girl

Love your hair?

    Don't mess with Baby Bear!

Note from the Poet:

In the fairy tale, I always get the idea that Baby Bear is so sweet and innocent. But I wanted to go against that idea. I decided to make Baby Bear kind of tough—or at least trying to sound like he's tough!

SNOW WHITE AND THE SEVEN DWARVES

Magic mirror told the truth

Queen could not compete with youth

No longer fairest in the land,

"Kill Snow White!" was Queen's command

Snow White fled through wooded glen

Found shelter with some mini-men

Poison apple dropped her, dead,

'Til Prince's kiss brought life, instead

Note from the Poet:

It's so hard to summarize a pretty complicated story in a few lines. I started out by outlining the main plot points of Snow White:

1.   The mirror insults the Queen.

2.   The Queen orders Snow White killed.

3.   Snow White hides out with the dwarves.

4.   The Queen kills Snow White with the poison apple.

5.   The Prince brings her back to life with a kiss.

I tried to write the poem in 5 lines, but I couldn't fit in enough detail. In the end, I was happy with 8 lines.

Would It Kill You to Lie a Little?
Item for sale: Magic mirror
For sale by: The Evil Queen

mirror

crass   glass

staring sharing uncaring

harsh - talking,   face - mocking

knowing showing crowing

stated   hated

truth

Note from the Poet:

Diamantes usually feature opposites that are each described for exactly half of the poem, but this is an unconventional diamante. When I look at is now that it's finished, I realize that lines 2-5 all really describe the mirror, and only line 6 describes truth, the final line. The Queen sees both the mirror and the truth as her enemies, I think, and this poem shows that.

Touched by Snow White

Item for sale: Keepsakes from Snow White's visit
For sale by: The Seven Dwarves

Snow White was an angel,

so sweet and so kind.

It pains us to sell the things she left behind.

But we've mined all the diamonds.

We're quite short on cash,

so we're forced to get rid of our souvenir stash:

The pillow she drooled on each night as she slept;

The actual broom that she held when she swept up our
cottage;

Her slippers;

A sweet note she wrote;

And the brown chunk of apple we popped from her throat!

Note from the Poet:

When somebody is famous, all their friends seem to
want to get in on the action, the fame, the money. So I
thought that maybe when the dwarves' mine ran out,
they would try to sell off some of the things Snow
White had touched. This makes me a little sad,
actually, because I don't want them to be false friends.
But...this is what came out, so I guess somewhere in
my brain, I believe that they would do this.

Don't Call It a Coffin!
Item for sale: Glass coffin
For sale by: The Prince

A prison of glass.

I first saw her face,

Frozen, but beautiful,

Sweetened by grace.

But now we're downsizing—

We need some more space!

Make it a piggy bank.

Fill it with fish.

Fill it with nacho chips.

Use as a dish.

Do what you want!

Do whatever you wish!

It's comfy enough for an

Afternoon snooze.

And the price is so low

you can hardly refuse.

So help us recycle!

Reduce and reuse!

Note from the Poet:

I had a blast trying to come up with other things you could use a glass coffin for: a piggy bank, a fish tank, a chip/dip bowl, a serving dish.... Some ideas I brainstormed but discarded are a phone booth, a bathtub, and a pet bed.

RAPUNZEL

Rapunzel wailed,

frightened, trapped

inside a tower.

She unwrapped

her golden hair

to form a stair.

Prince climbed up

to kiss her there.

Witch discovered

Prince's trick.

She pushed.

He fell upon a stick.

Blind until

Rapunzel's voice

repaired his sight.

Rejoice! Rejoice!

...but then

Note from the Poet:

All I remembered about Rapunzel was the hair. Until I went back to re-read the fairy tale, I didn't know/recall that the prince was blinded. Wow! Fairy tales are so violent, and I always think it's funny how they've become so popular for kids.

No Use for Ribbons
Item for sale: Ribbons
For sale by: Rapunzel

Grosgrain ribbons—

>Two per quarter!

Hair once flowing

>Now is shorter.

Long blonde locks

>Used as ladder

Gave me headaches,

>Made me madder

Than the Prince,

>who's quite appalled.

He hasn't called

>Since I went bald!

Note from the Poet:

I learn new words all the time while reading, and as a writer, I like to use a word here and there my reader might not know. I always want to know how words came about, how they are pronounced, etc. The word "grosgrain" is a French word that means "coarse texture." Grosgrain ribbons look like they have little ridges on them. It's pronounced grow-grain. In French, the letter s is always (or at least almost always) silent.

This Diamond Sparkles Like Her Shiny, Bald Head
Item for sale: Wedding ring
For sale by: The Prince, who kind of wishes his sight
had not been restored

Did you see?

She chopped her hair off!

Now the sun creates a glare off

of her scalp. This look would scare off

anyone who wasn't blind.

What to do?

I try to stare off

far away. Will my pain wear off?

I don't know! This makes me swear off

every girl, all womankind!

Note from the Poet:

Sometimes one poem grows right out of another! When Rapunzel sold off her hair ribbons, I wondered how her prince would feel about that. As you can tell, I decided that her husband would not be all that happy!

Charming Castle – Perfect for One
Item for sale: Castle
For sale by: The Witch

One room

One window

Not one single door

No rugs

No curtains

No tacky décor

I'm old

Can't climb up

These walls made of stone

So make me

An offer

And make this your home!

Note from the Poet:

Repetition (I've talked about this before, so I'm repeating myself!) is key to lots of poetry. I repeat two words here: "one" and "no." The castle where Rapunzel was kept is a lonely place without comfort or luxury. Repeating those words helps get that idea across.

JACK AND THE BEANSTALK

Jack's mother gave a cow to Jack
To sell and bring the money back

When he came home with beans, she frowned
And flung them down onto the ground

A beanstalk grew,
and Jack, defiant,
Climbed the sky-high vine to giant

Jack stole gold, a hen, and harp,

Then chopped
  the plant
    with axe-blade
      sharp

Note from the Poet:

This is a "don't do this" Note. Sometimes, a poet changes the natural word order to make rhymes work. Look at the last five lines. If you were talking, you'd say, "Jack stole gold, a hen, and harp, then chopped the plant with a sharp axe blade." But that doesn't rhyme. So I put axe-blade before sharp. You can get away with it once in a great while, but it makes the reader have to stop and think, so avoid it if you can!

Fee-Fie-Foe-Fairian: Surprise! I'm Vegetarian!
Item for sale: Ogre's knife
For sale by: The Ogre

Take my knife!

I've got no meat!

I can't have

more boys to eat!

Peeled or boiled,

served on toast,

kids were what I

loved the *most*!

Doc said, "Giant!

Watch your diet!"

Nag, nag, nag.

·I said I'd try it.

Juicy apples—

crunchy, fresh...

But...

I'm still craving

human flesh.

Run along!

Beat it! Shoo!

Or I'll use my knife

and fork on YOU!

Note from the Poet:

Sometimes, I just have a gross sense of humor, and that's what I'm showcasing in this poem. Can you imagine if a vicious giant had to stop eating meat? I love that idea!

Solid Gold Sounds
Item for sale: Golden harp
For sale by: The Ogre's wife

This magic, gargantuan, glorious harp

Forms notes that float golden, mournful, and sharp

Some shoppers have told me the price seems too high,

But I've masses, I've *mountains* of veggies to buy

My husband eats 2 tons of produce each day

At a protein-packed broccoli-and-spinach buffet

He's simply voracious since giving up meats

And I have to pay for the food that he eats

I'm sad that he doesn't eat kids anymore--

We paid a lot less for our groceries before!

Note from the Poet:

When poets work on meter, we use symbols like this: -/--/--/--/ Each / is a stressed beat. Each – is an unstressed beat. My last line was "Our grocery bill was much cheaper before!" But the meter, or beat, doesn't quite work perfectly. Here's how that last couplet looks, before and after:

before:

I'm-SAD-that-he-DOES-n't-eat-KIDS-a-ny-MORE

our-GROCE-ry-BILL-was-much-CHEA-per-be-FORE

-/--/--/--/

-/-/--/--/

after:

I'm-SAD-that-he-DOES-n't-eat-KIDS-a-ny-MORE

we-PAID-a-lot-LESS-for-our-GROCE-ries-be-FORE

-/--/--/--/

-/--/--/--/

The World's Last Magic Bean
Item for sale: One bean
For sale by: Jack

One bean

hidden away.

I want to plant magic,

but my mother would have a cow.

Dare you!

A Note from the Poet:

Do you know the phrase "Don't have a cow"? When I was a kid, "have a cow" was slang for "get all upset." So we would say things like, "My mom'll have a cow if I don't unload the dishwasher." Saying, "Don't have a cow" to someone was like saying, "Chill out. No big deal." When I wrote this cinquain (a poem with 5 lines of 2-4-6-8-2 syllables), I had fun playing with literal vs. figurative. Literally, the mom wants to have a cow in exchange for the money. But Jack has bought a bean instead. And figuratively, he knows his mom would be super upset if he planted another magic bean.

THE EMPEROR'S NEW CLOTHES

The emperor loved high fashion,
Raw silk, and velvet with passion.

Two tailors vowed to provide
Exquisite clothes, but they lied.

They spun make-believe on their looms,
Stitched invisible tassels and plumes.

"Only dummies can not see our clothes!
Our robes and our silk ruffled bows!"

So the emperor paid them their loot
And strode down the street in his

(birthday)   suit!

A Note from the Poet:

I talked about meter or rhythm being important. In
this poem, though, I purposely broke the meter. The
ending of the poem would have perfect meter if it said:

So the emperor paid them their loot

And strode down the street in his suit!

By adding in (birthday), I ruin the meter. But I do it on purpose! I want the reader to get a little tangled up and pause and get the joke. The emperor is in his birthday suit (naked—gasp), not a suit of fine fabric.

Fashion Fit for a King!
Item for sale: Clothing and fabrics
For sale by: The traveling clothmakers—Contact us for
your next gala event!

Ruby robes! Threads of gold.

Rarely seen, rarely sold!

Feel the velvet! Come adore these

Sumptuous clothes the ruler wore.

Jeweled slippers for your feet!

Fashion for the true elite!

Nothing there? Only air?

Not much for a man to wear?

Don't you see? They're in full view--

Except to silly fools like you!

A Note from the Poet:

I strongly dislike pushy salespeople. If I go into a store
and someone hovers over me and talks at me, I leave. I
pictured the traveling clothmakers as very pushy
salespeople. Their skill is in persuasion, not in
clothing making.

Seeing Is Overrated
Item for sale: Glasses
For sale by: The boy who told the truth

I will never—no, not ever!—

put my glasses on again.

I was weeding in the garden.

I heard trumpets call, and then

the king marched slowly past me

wearing nothing but his crown!

The king! Parading naked

through the center of the town!

I said, "He has no clothes on!"

Used my hands to shield my eyes

but I could not block the image of

his belly, chest, and thighs.

He was dirty and quite furry

and he scratched like he had fleas,

and the odor as he waddled by

was strangely close to cheese.

I should have kept my mouth shut—

but instead I told the truth.

All the grown-ups gasped in horror,

murmured, "Stupid, foolish youth!"

So lend your ears if you don't want

to be locked up like me!

Next time you spy a naked king,

pretend that you don't see!

A Note from the Poet:

One night, during the time I was working on this poetry collection, I did a goofy dance in front of my kids. One of my daughters cried, "My eyes! They burn!" We say that a fair amount, actually, when we see something we wish we hadn't. And that made me think about a poor kid who saw the naked emperor. You can't unsee something horrible. Unfortunately.

Bathrobe, Slightly Tight
Item for sale: Bathrobe
For sale by: The Emperor, aka The King

It's pink as sunsets in the west

with ducklings stitched across the chest.

It's warm and fuzzy—it's the best,

especially if you're—oops—undressed!

A Note from the Poet:

This is one of my favorite images. I picture the naked emperor, suddenly realizing he really *is* naked, running to cover himself with his favorite ducky bathrobe.

THUMBELINA

A woman planted barley corn.

From magic seed, a child was born.

Sweet—and tiny as your thumb!

She drank up dew and dined on crumb.

Girl escaped a lonely toad.

She met a giant bird and rode

upon his back to pint-sized prince.

And she's been happy ever since!

A Note from the Poet:

Sometimes a poem describes something I know I won't ever be able to really do, even though I wish I could. In this poem, it's flying on a bird's back. Wouldn't it be cool to sail through the sky on the steady, smooth back of a bird? And you wouldn't even have to do any work! It would be kind of like the giant swings at theme parks. Sigh. I would like to do that. But I can't, so I put it in a poem.

Outgrown
Item for sale: Walnut bed
For sale by: Thumbelina

My toes hang off

My walnut bed

My acorn cap

Won't fit my head

My leafy belt's

Begun to pinch

I've grown a whopping

Quarter-inch!

A Note from the Poet:

When I was a kid, I loved making homes and clothes
for tiny, imaginary creatures and fairies. A pea pod
could be a canoe, a pencil was a giant spear, and a few
shoeboxes turned into mansions. I had fun thinking
about what Thumbelina would sleep in and wear.

Daisy Petal Wedding Gown—Unused
Item for sale: Daisy Petal Wedding Gown
For sale by: The Toad

My mother brought me home a bride

    (Don't laugh—

    She has lovely taste)

Delicate, perfect Thumbelina made my webbed feet quiver

    But she left

I wove reeds and marigolds into the tidiest nest for her

    But she left

Spiders spun her a wedding dress of silk and sunlight

    But she left

She saw only

my dry skin

    (I am a toad, after all.

    What did she expect?

    The slimy moistness of a frog?)

and my flat, black eyes

    (Come on.

    You can't help

    the eyes you're born with.)

There was love inside me

(You probably see where this is going, right?)

But she left

A Note from the Poet:

I wanted a sad refrain here, because when you're heart-broken, you sometimes just keep repeating the same thing over and over again. "But she left" sounds so sad and final to me, so I used it four times in the poem. I love being able to use it for the very last line.

Fixer-Upper Fly Wings

Item for sale: Wings
For sale by: The Fairy Prince

With glassy wings

    from two white flies,

my sweetie soared,

    explored the skies.

She flew too high

    then spiraled, crashed.

Her dainty wings

    were slightly trashed.

But they aren't ruined!

One drop of glue

    will fix them up

    as good as new!

A Note from the Poet:

Finding just the right word is what poetry is all about. Sometimes I'll write a poem very quickly—this first draft took 10 minutes. But then I nit-pick words. Some wrong words messed up the beat or didn't have the exact meaning I wanted, like "glassy." Before I got to that word, I tried "see-through," "clear," "delicate," "shiny," and "stained glass."

COME AGAIN NEXT YEAR!

Did you peek at Thumbelina?
Did you meet the witch?
Did you see Rapunzel's head?
Did you make her rich?

Careful with that magic bean.
Double-check that clock.
Are you sure your doll will fit
That teeny-tiny frock?

Tomorrow this will disappear,
So every shopper learns:
It's good to try before you buy
'Cause we don't take returns!

See ya next year!

A Note from the Poet:

This poem was inspired by my niece after I went to the theme park. "Did you ride the roller coaster?" she asked. "Did you eat cotton candy? Did you go on the swings?" I loved that energy. I could hear her voice in my head as I wrote the opening stanza.

ABOUT THE EDUCATOR: COLBY SHARP

Colby Sharp is a husband, dad, and a third grade teacher. He helps run Nerdy Book Club.

Visit his blog:
mrcolbysharp.com

Check out Nerdy Book Club:
nerdybookclub.wordpress.com/

Follow him on Twitter:
@ColbySharp

Follow him on Instagram:
instagram.com/colbysharp

Follow him on Pinterest:
pinterest.com/colbysharp/

Addendum from Laura Purdie Salas: If you follow Colby Sharp on any kind of social media at all, you can't help but notice his enthusiasm, his real passion, for books and teaching. One thing he does not really have a passion for, however, is poetry. When I asked if he might be interested in contributing activities, he wrote: "I'd love to play along. Poetry REALLY stresses me out, so I may not be of much help, but I'm always up for trying!" I don't know if creating these activities led him one step closer to being a poetry convert, but I hope so. I was really excited to have an educator who WASN'T already a poetry lover contribute to this 30 Painless Classroom Poems series.

Mr. Colby Sharp is exactly the kind of teacher I'm doing these books for—someone who deeply loves books, kids, and teaching, but who gets a panicky feeling, perhaps a deer in the headlights look, when you ask him to teach poetry. So I hope you'll enjoy his activities for these poems—I sure did!

CLASSROOM ACTIVITY GUIDE

1. Have students create a newspaper ad to promote the garage sale of a character from a book they love. Be sure to include words and pictures. They could also try this for a different character. Maybe even the antagonist.

2. Using an audio capture app, have students create a 30-second commercial encouraging people to come to the garage sale of your favorite fairy tale character. For extra fun; have kids pretend that they are that character.

3. Have students draw an outline of the yard sale of a book character. Encourage them to think about what that character's yard would look like and what items might be included in their yard sale.

4. Pretending that they are a character from a fairy tale, have students write about which fairy tale character's garage sale from a different fairy tale they'd like to shop at. Encourage them to include the items that their character would want to buy. For instance, maybe Thumbelina would like to buy Snow White's coffin to use as a giant swimming pool.

5. Tell students that they are going to have a garage sale this weekend, and everything they own is going to be put up for sale. Have them write about which fairy tale character would most want to shop at their family's garage sale. Explain.

6. It's Rare! It's Bear! My Price Is Fair! - On the National Geographic website or other news archive, kids can read about the 4,000-year-old bowl of noodles found in China. Discuss how scientists figured out what the noodles were made of, and talk about the importance of close observation in scientific exploration. If you're brave, you could even let several food items like bread, pasta, and peanut butter dry out in bowls or on plates for several weeks in a secret location. Then let students examine their archaeological finds and note details to try to figure out exactly what kind of food each one is.

7. Would It Kill You to Lie a Little? - Bring an old mirror with a peeling back to class and demonstrate how the glass itself does not reflect (just like a window). It's the metallic film behind the glass that makes the reflection.

8. Jack and the Beanstalk - Provide students with a small plastic bag, a paper towel, a lima bean and a little bit of water. Have students soak the paper towel, use it to wrap the bean, and then tape it to a classroom window. After a couple of weeks, take the seedlings off the window and have students make observations.

9. This Diamond Sparkles Like Her Shiny, Bald Head - Share with students the Mohs Scale of Hardness. Provide them with a bag of various types of rocks and have them give each rock the scratch test to determine which rocks have the greatest hardness.

10. Come Again Next Year - Have students write a letter to next year's version of themselves. Have them include goals, their favorite things to do, etc. Have students place their letter in an envelope and address it to themselves. Set a reminder in your calendar to mail the letters in exactly one year. You could also use an online tool like FutureMe to have students do this in email form.

11. Fixer-Upper Fly Wings - With a camera or a sketch book, have students head to the schoolyard to explore the creators that inhabit their playground. Students may share their findings when they return to class.

12. Out of Time - Have students create a sundial with a paper plate and a straw. Have students poke a hole in the center of the plate and insert the straw. A few minutes before noon, take the students outside and have them place their sundials on the ground. At noon have them locate where the straw's shadow falls on the paper plate. Have them mark the end of that shadow, on the plate, with a 12. Repeat steps at 1, 2, and 3. Have students predict where the shadow will fall at other hours of the day.

13. Up in Flames - Have students call the local fire department and invite them to school for a visit. Before the visit, have students research fire safety. When the firefighters come to school, have students present their findings to the firefighters. This will be a fun change, as firefighters are usually the ones doing the fire safety presentations.

14. Fee-Fie-Foe-Fairian: Surprise! I'm Vegetarian! - Encourage each student to bring in enough of one fruit or vegetable for each student in the class to have a sample for a taste testing day. During the taste testing, have students try as many fruits and vegetables as they like. Have them record their thoughts of each vegetable for them to share at home with their family.

15. The Emperor's New Clothes - Have students dress up as a favorite book character for the day. Each student can try and guess which character their classmates picked.

--Colby Sharp

SCHOOL VISITS

Laura Purdie Salas loves to visit schools and work with students and/or teachers! She is available for both in-person and Skype visits, and she presents at conferences, book festivals, story times, and professional development events, as well. Her approach is to make books and reading and writing fun and inviting for students. For educators, her focus is on demystifying the writing or reading process and giving practical tips for incorporating poetry into the classroom setting. For more information, please explore the Presentations area of her website: laurasalas.com/present.html

THE BOOKS IN THE 30 PAINLESS CLASSROOM POEMS SERIES

Here are the first six books in the 30 Painless Classroom Poems series. For a complete, up-to-date listing, please visit 30PainlessClassroomPoems.com

What's Inside? Poems to Explore the Park
Fifteen couplet questions answered by 15 quatrain response poems (all rhyming) explore common objects found at the park, from pine cones to puddles to baseballs. Photo illustrated.

Sample:

What's inside of this tiny cocoon?
This soft, silky, fuzzy, white, paper balloon?

Caterpillar started out, spring green and bright,
It's changing to moth, it's arriving quite soon
With pale wings to flutter through silvery night
And flash in the path of the cool distant moon

Riddle-ku: (Haiku) Poems for Very Close Reading

Haiku riddles told from the point of view of everyday objects challenge students to read closely for clues and context. Photo illustrated.

Sample:

I dive into milk
It's my start-the-day routine:

Swimming with my friends

Answer: cereal

A Need to Feed: Predator and Prey Poems

These rhyming poems on the prowl are in many forms but are all narrated from the point of view of predators talking about their hunting methods. In each poem, the final word is the name of the prey animal. Each poem also has a brief prose note (in addition to the Note from the Poet) about the poem's topic.

Sample:
Saltwater Crocodile (Saltie)

I'm king of Australia. I'm top crocodile.
I'm a leather-skinned ton
And a razor blade smile.

I skulk in the river, just 12 inches deep,
I'm a 20-foot hulk--
You might think I'm asleep.

An oinker gets thirsty. I rocket--I lunge!
I lock down my jaws
For our dark, salty plunge.

I roll in the deep 'til its huge heart stops beating,
Then carve up the meat
'Til it's just right for eating.

I swim toward the swamp on the opposite shore,
Cleaning my teeth with a tusk of wild _____

Boar.

Note: The saltwater crocodile waits in shallow river water for animals to drink from or try to cross the river. Then it bursts out, grabs its prey, and drags it into the river to drown it in a death roll. It does not actually use the boar's tusk to clean its teeth, though!

Fairy Tale Garage Sale: Poems of After Ever After

This collection of poems (mostly rhyming, but different forms/meters) imagines that all the characters in Fairy Tale Land are getting rid of their junk. Each poem is a "sales flyer" for a certain object from that character's story.

Sample:

Item for sale: Ball gowns
For sale by: Cinderella's stepsisters

Beautiful Gowns Too Good for You

Buy our gowns, our shoes, our jewels.
Buy them all, you stupid fools.

We tried them all--they didn't work!
The Prince chose *her*. He's such a jerk.

Why-ku: (Haiku) Poems of Wonder About the Natural World

Fifteen pairs of haiku ask and try to answer questions about the natural world.

Sample:

I can never tell
if clouds will cancel practice
or stay high and dry.

Why Do Clouds Only Sometimes Rain?

Each cloud lugs raindrops
like hefty backpacks--drops them
when they're too heavy.

Wacky, Wild, and Wonderful: 50 State Poems

Each poem celebrates one natural, geographical, cultural, or historical aspect of a state. The poems are a mix of rhyming and non-rhyming and many poetic forms. Each poem also has a brief prose note (in addition to the Note from the Poet) about the poem's topic. Photo illustrated.

Sample:

New Jersey: At the Shore

summer
crowded, noisy
splashing, jostling, shouting
boardwalks, sunscreen, go-carts, ice cream
packing, leaving, memories fading
empty, still
autumn

Note: The east coast of New Jersey, along the Atlantic Ocean, is called the Jersey Shore or simply The Shore. Millions of people visit towns along this 125-mile long length of shoreline, and many families have long traditions of spending the entire summer at the shore. The seaside towns all up and down the coast cater to visitors and tourists, with boardwalks, amusement parks, golf courses, and, of course, the beach. All summer, the mood is festive and noisy. But after Labor Day, when all the families have returned home, the carnival rides are shuttered until the next year, and the Jersey Shore settles into its quiet, off-season mood of natural beauty. [Diamante]

INVITATION TO SHARE YOUR STORIES

Hi, educators! I'd love to hear from you about how you use the poems and activities in this book. If you'd be willing to let me share your stories, pictures, lesson plans, etc., publicly, please email me at Laura@30PainlessClassroomPoems.com. I hope to eventually have a section on my website full of teacher-created materials.

And if you enjoyed this book, I'd be incredibly grateful if you'd rate/review it on Amazon. Even a very brief review helps the book reach more people. Thank you for spreading the poetry love!

--Laura

CREDITS AND INFO

[Any images not listed were either taken by Laura Purdie Salas or are stock photos/illustrations purchased by Laura and used within the restrictions of that purchase.]

Moon image used in the background on the dedication page obtained from Ryan and Sarah Deeds on Flickr, shared under a Creative Commons Generic license: https://creativecommons.org/licenses/by-sa/2.0/

Timeline created using NCTE's interactive tool at ReadWriteThink.org.

Timeline images:

Light bulb: Bombeta de Llum (Wikimedia Commons, public domain)

Teen Cinderella: Crysco Photography on flickr

Laughing girl: C. Szeto on flickr

Ebay logo: "EBay logo" by eBay / Adrian Frutiger (typeface) - eBay: A new look. Licensed under public domain via Wikimedia Commons

Garage sale signs: J on flickr

Crossed fingers: By Evan-Amos (Own work) [CC-BY-SA-3.0 (http://creativecommons.org/licenses/by-sa/3.0)], via Wikimedia Commons

Sad face: Jgsho (Own work) [CC-BY-SA-3.0 (http://creativecommons.org/licenses/by-sa/3.0)], via Wikimedia Commons

Happy face: Ramesh NG (Flickr: Smileyes) [CC-BY-SA-2.0 (http://creativecommons.org/licenses/by-sa/2.0)], via Wikimedia Commons

Nancie Atwell quotation from a talk about *Naming the World: A Year in Poems*, accessed 9/12/14 at http://www.namingtheworld.com/#

Photo of Laura Purdie Salas by Katherine Warde

Photo of Colby Sharp by Colby Sharp

Made in the USA
San Bernardino, CA
29 November 2014